Sprinkled with Kindness
Written by Benjamin Lee
Illustrated by Kathleen Lee

Copyright © 2021 by Benjamin Lee

All rights reserved.

No part of this book may be scanned, uploaded, reproduced, distributed, or transmitted in any form or by any means, electronic, or mechanical, including photocopying and recording, or by any information storage and retrieval system, without permission in writing from the copyright owner.

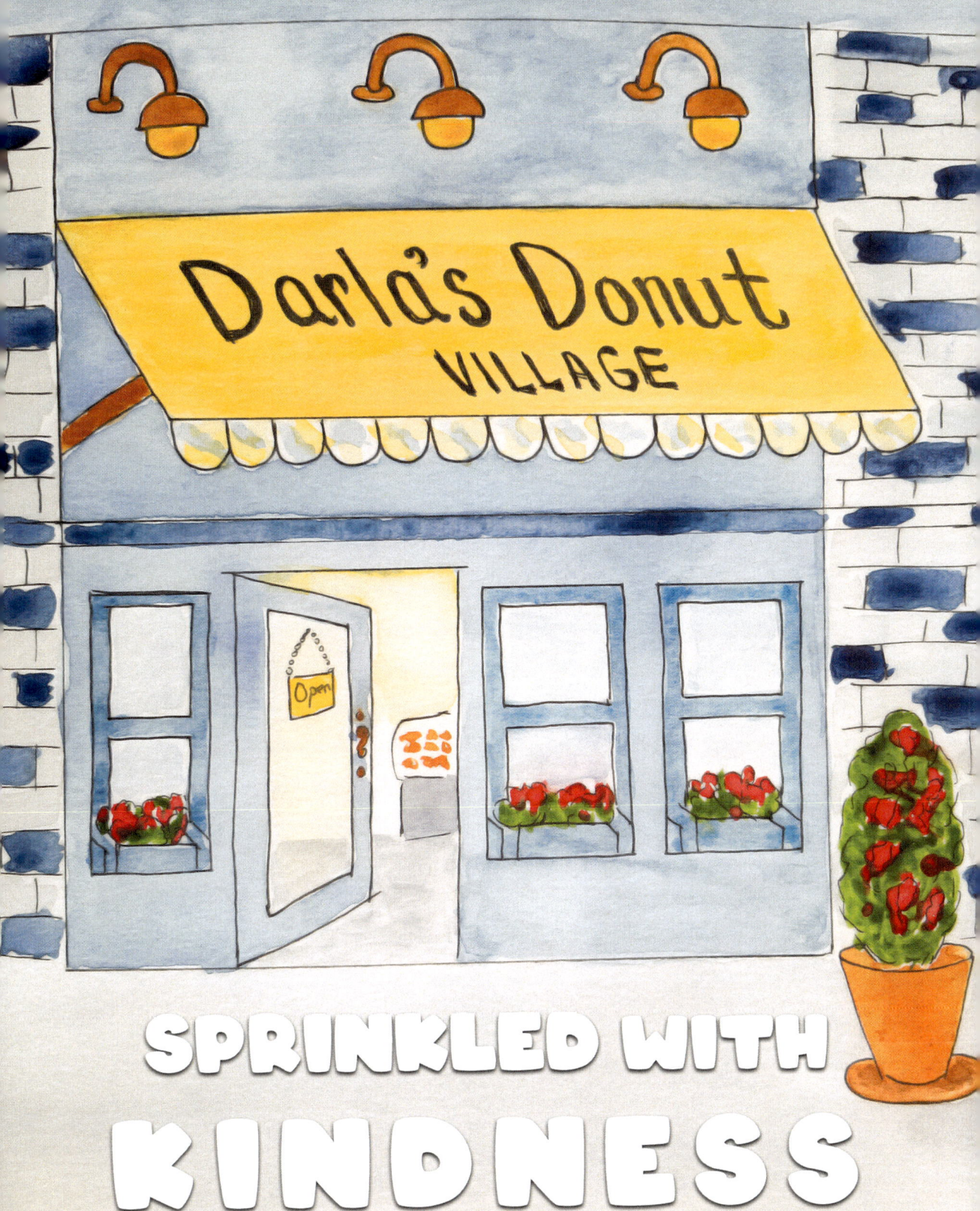

Hi, everyone! It's Glaze again.
Do you remember me?

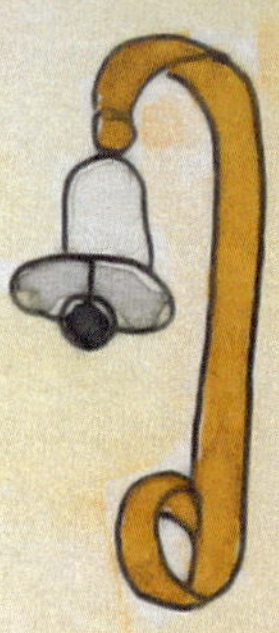

I'm still living at Darla's Donut Village,
and I'm happy as can be!

"I don't remember. I am a new donut here."

My life has changed since I learned that I have good dough inside!

I'm now giddy to dip in the plain glaze after being fried.

Darla even shines a spotlight on me to show me off a bit.

Oh! How wonderful my glaze sparkles when it is lit!

I almost forgot.
Meet our new friend,
Barry Blue!

"I would love that."

Let me tell you a recent story, Barry, so you can learn more about our crew.

Since the donut critic came in to see me,
I've even been in the news!

YouTubers came rushing in to pose
with me to increase their video views.

Well, I used to be extra careful to keep my dough and glaze super smooth and clean.

Sprink wasn't so careful, spreading her sprinkles of pink, blue, yellow, and green.

EARLIER THAT DAY...

Sometimes as donuts, we get
our frostings mixed and sprinkled.

Sprink needed to be more careful since donuts get put
in the "Day-Old" pile when messy and crinkled.

She just twirled around the shop,
bumping into all of us.

She's loved for her sprinkles
and didn't understand the fuss.

The other day, Sprink went to take her rainbow sprinkle shower.

All the other donuts that were tired of getting sprinkled met me by the flour.

Cru was passed up by a customer
because he was speckled in red.

He asked us to come up with a plan
to help stop the color spread.

Long John said he knew
how to keep Sprink away.

They could all hide when she
came out to play.

Just then Sprink came out of the sugary shower looking for the other donuts.

The only one she found was the old, vanilla cake donut with peanuts.

Sprink took a dip in the oil and rolled
in the frosting to pass the time.

None of the other donuts could be found
when Darla turned the "Open" sign.

The next day, no one would play
with her again and she got teary eyed.

All the donuts kept their distance
from Sprink, even when she cried.

"That isn't nice at all."

Darla was quick to see what was happening with her yummy, fried treats.

People don't visit her shop because she serves perfectly looking eats.

It was more important to Darla that
the pastries accept each other and be kind.

It took her only 'til the end of the day
to come up with a way to remind.

THE GOLDEN-BROWN RULE

There was a sign on the wall the next morning that read, "The Golden-Brown Rule."

Darla boxed all the donuts, putting them in rows and lines like children at school.

"This new rule isn't a test to see which of you
sweet treats has been bad.

It is posted as a reminder to be kind
and help others from feeling sad."

"The trick is to always treat everyone around you very well.

A happy donut always gets chosen because customers can tell."

All the donuts knew they had been
unkind to their friend Sprink.

I walked over to Sprink's side of the box
and picked up a sprinkle that was pink.

I gently placed the sprinkle
on my soft, sugary glaze.

Customers visit the donut shop
and love us in so many ways.

They don't crave Darla's donuts because we're perfect.

This shows it is more important to be kind and show respect.

We hear the bell as a darling, little customer walks in.

We all know and love her,
it's bright-eyed Winnie Lynn.

By now, all of the donut friends had placed sprinkles on their glaze and basically everywhere.

Sprink received so much support that it became a party with sprinkles thrown into the air!

Winnie Lynn's bright eyes lit up
more than we've ever seen before.

She loved all the donuts with sprinkles
so much she bought twenty-four!

The Golden-Brown Rule won't be hanging
on every wall where we go.

But now we know being kind increases the
bounce and flavor of our dough.

DARLA'S DONUTS VOTED BEST DONUT SHOP!

If you want to become the most delicious donut out there, then live by the rule and treat others with kindness and care!

DONUT HUG TIME

Sprinkle someone with kindness today!

About the author

Benjamin Lee, also known as "The Donut Critic" to many, has a deep love for desserts. His mission has been to bring happiness to others through positive and sweet messages. He fulfills this mission through his social accounts and as a Co-founder to Utah's largest dessert festival, Sugar High. Benjamin resides in Lehi, UT with his wife and four kids. He studied business and marketing at the University of Utah and received his MBA from Utah State University.

About the illustrator

Kathleen Lee can most often be found behind the lense of her camera, or with a paintbrush in her hand. She finds joy in teaching the arts to others helping them feel creative and successful. She has worked with children of all ages all her life, whether in employment or volunteer work. Kathleen has ten children of her own and 45 grandchildren. She studied business at the University of Utah, and more recently has studied Fine Arts at Dixie State University.

Made in the USA
Middletown, DE
25 November 2022

15952371R00024